Have you ever heard of

Quentin

Question

Mark?

Did you know that he is

the **nosiest** of the Puncs?

He never stops

asking questions –

which is why he is

a Customs Officer.

You will not be surprised to learn (will you?)

that he was a

nosy parker from

the day he was born.

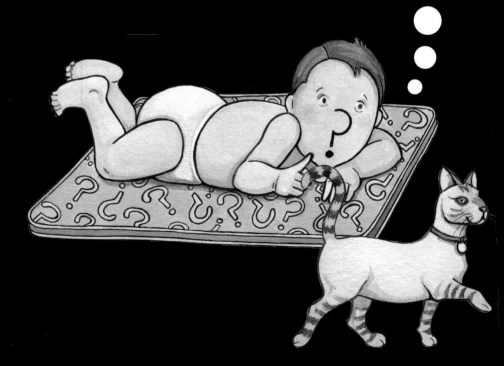

His very
first words were:

You may be
wondering who his
parents are?

Can you spare
a moment?

His mother, Wygelia, works
for PP.
What is that? you may ask.
(It means 'Punc Polls'.)

She stops people in the street and asks them silly questions, such as:

"How many chocolate biscuits did you eat for breakfast?"

"How often do you change your toothbrush?"

What about his father?

He is called Wyvern and he works for a magazine called **Punc Life**. He writes quizzes which ask tricky questions, such as:

"Who was the first Punc to fly over the Alps in a hang-glider?"

Punc Life

You've guessed (haven't you?) that Wyvern goes hang-gliding at weekends.

All through Quentin's childhood, Wyvern and Wygelia were worn out by his endless questions. Whenever they tried to watch their favourite TV show, **Who wants to be a Punc?**, he didn't give them a moment's peace.

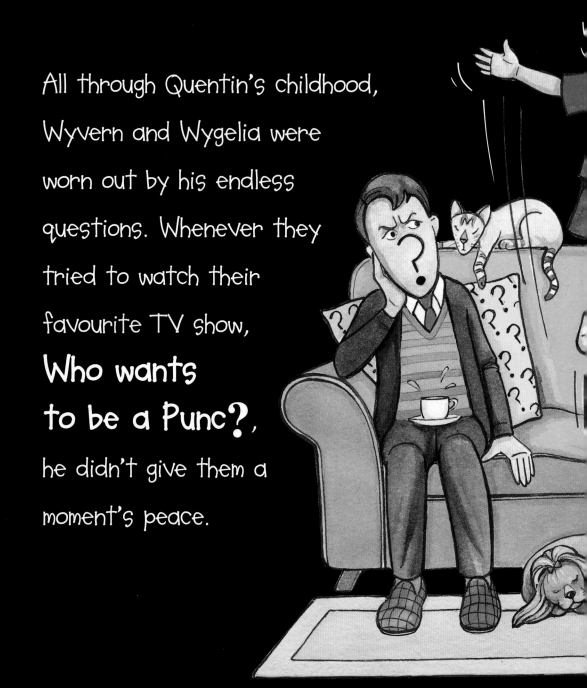

"What have we done to deserve this?"

they would ask each other as Quentin jumped up and down on the sofa, shouting:

"Who's that?"

"What's he doing?"

"Where's he gone?"

At school Quentin drove everyone mad with his questions. Every time he put up his hand in class, his teachers would mumble 'oh no' under their breath, and his friends would groan as he piped up:

"Why did King Puncotex break his neck?"

"Where does Space end?"

It's not surprising that he often suffers from a sore throat, is it?

Every morning when Quentin was going off to school, Wygelia would stand at the front door with a list of questions:

"Did you wash your hands?"

"Have you cleaned your teeth?"

"Where have you put your dinner money?"

Have you noticed that Quentin is rather pasty-faced?

Perhaps you'd like to know why?

It's because he isn't a bit sporty. Instead, he likes to sit indoors with his stamp collection.

(There's nothing wrong with that, is there?)

"I wonder where Alapalapunc is?"

No doubt by now you've gathered that being an airport Customs Officer suits Quentin in every way?

He spends all day long indoors staring passengers straight in the eye and asking them:

"Have you read this notice, Madam?"

"What have you got to declare?"

"Did you pack this bag yourself, Sir?"

Sometimes he pounces on passengers and makes them open their baggage.

He shuffles things around and picks things up (which is why he wears white gloves) and asks:

"What have you got in here?"

"Where did you buy it?"

"What did you pay for it?"

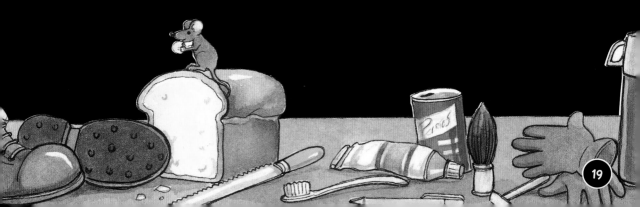

Sometimes he just stares and doesn't speak at all.

Can you guess why?

Could it be because he has just found a **snake** in someone's sponge bag?

You may want to know if Quentin has a wife?

Well, he has. She is called Wyandotte (Dotty for short).

Do you want to know where her name came from?

It was from her mother's great-great-great grandmother, a Native American from Wyoming.

All day long, Dotty drives people potty with her ceaseless questions:

"Why are you so late this morning?"

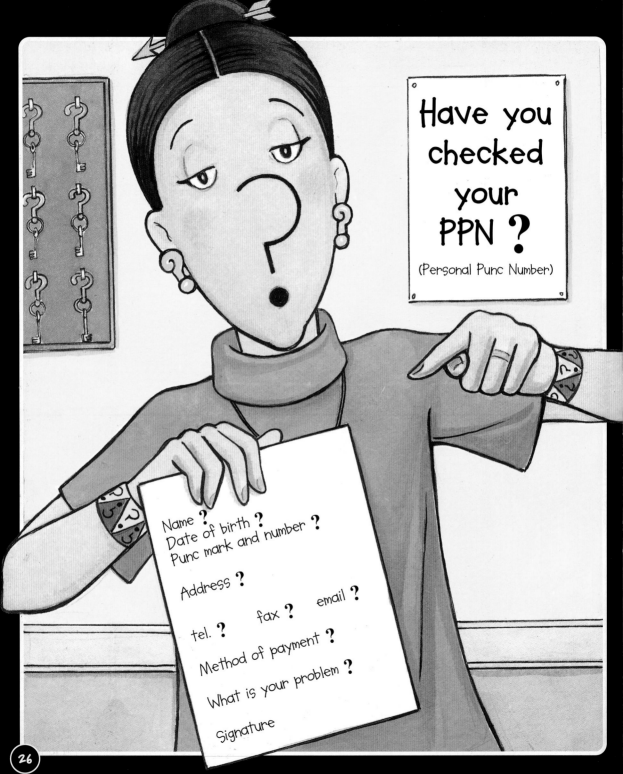

Can you guess what Dotty's job is?

She is a receptionist and spends most of her day helping visitors to fill in forms:

"What is your home address?"

"When is your date of birth?"

"Do you use a mobile phone?"

"How will you pay your bill?"

Why do you think that Quentin and Dotty have a very happy marriage?

It is because they just ask each other questions and don't bother about answers:

Dotty: "Have you had a good day?"

Quentin: "What's for supper?"

Dotty: "How's your sore thumb?"

Quentin: "What's wrong with the kettle?"

Do you know anyone quite like Dotty and Quentin?

Have you ever met anyone as curious as Quentin?

Wherever

and whenever

and however

there are questions to be asked,

you will find him –

won't you

? ? ?

Quentin's Checklist

- **Use a question mark (instead of a full stop) at the end of a sentence that asks a question, like this:**
  Have you ever heard of Quentin Question Mark?

- **Asking-words are all followed by a question mark:**
  Who? Why? What? Where? When?

- **Use a question mark when a sentence is half-statement and half-question:**
  You won't be surprised (will you?) that Quentin is a nosy parker.

- **You might find a question mark in brackets, expressing doubt about the word(s) it is placed after:**
  The 'Punc Times' was founded in 1901 (?)

- **Quiz books are full of questions – and question marks – which test your knowledge, like this:**
  Why did King Puncotex break his neck?

- **Teachers, as well as students, ask difficult questions:**
  How do you spell 'Alapalapunc'?

- **Doctors ask personal questions:**
  How much do you weigh?

- **People often ask questions when they argue:**
  Why should I? What do you mean? How could you?

- **In cartoons, comics and advertisements, you might see a row of question marks added for fun, or to make the question stand out:**
  "W-w-what's happening?????"

- **Again, especially in cartoons, a question mark might sit next to an exclamation mark, for impact:**
  "Are you crazy?!"

- **Remember:** Asking questions is good. It means that you are curious and like to find out about things. But asking silly questions, or too many questions can be very annoying, especially if you can't be bothered to listen to the answers.